Handel's Warthog Music

Nonsense in Music

The Peer Gynt Sweet

Drawings and Verses
by
Simon Drew

ANTIQUE COLLECTORS' CLUB

to
Caroline
and to the well known musicologists
john and sandi

First published 1993
© 1993 Simon Drew
World copyright reserved
Reprinted 1996

British Library Cataloguing in Publication Data
A catalogue record for this book is
available from the British Library

ISBN 1 85149 186 4

Published and printed in England by the Antique Collectors' Club Ltd.
Woodbridge, Suffolk IP12 1DS

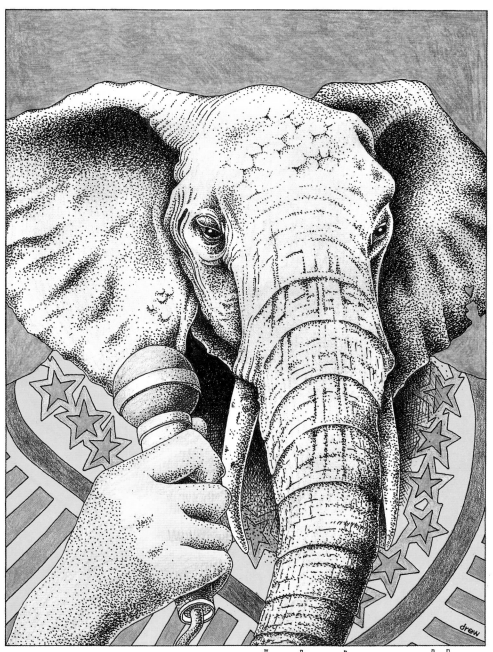

elephants gerald

wolf gang mows art

the elvis songbook:

are you loathsome
tonight?

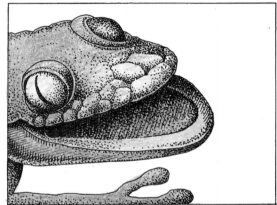

in the gecko

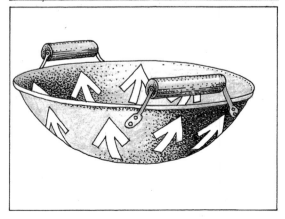

jailhouse wok

summertime – and delivering is easy ...

knight on a bear mountain

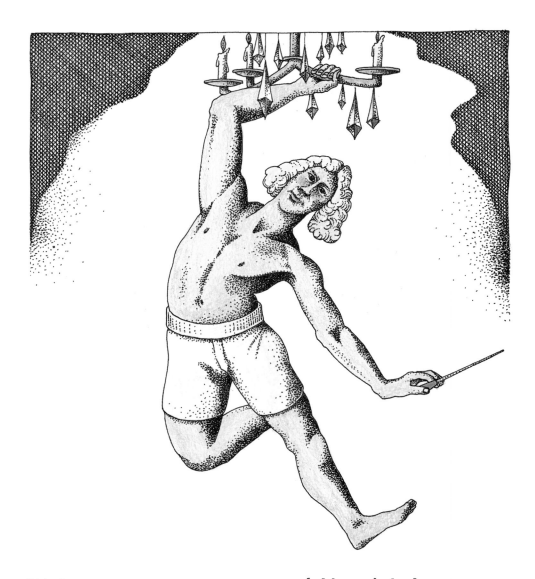

We have a composer named Handel - here;
he caused such a terrible scandal - dear.
When bored of some speeches
he pulled off his breeches
and swung on the best royal chandel - ier.

There was a composer named Haydn
who'd saddle his horse and go raydn.
The urge was so strong,
he'd ride for so long –
so causing his backside to waydn.

zadok: the piste

l'après midi d'un phone

I hurdle through the grapevine

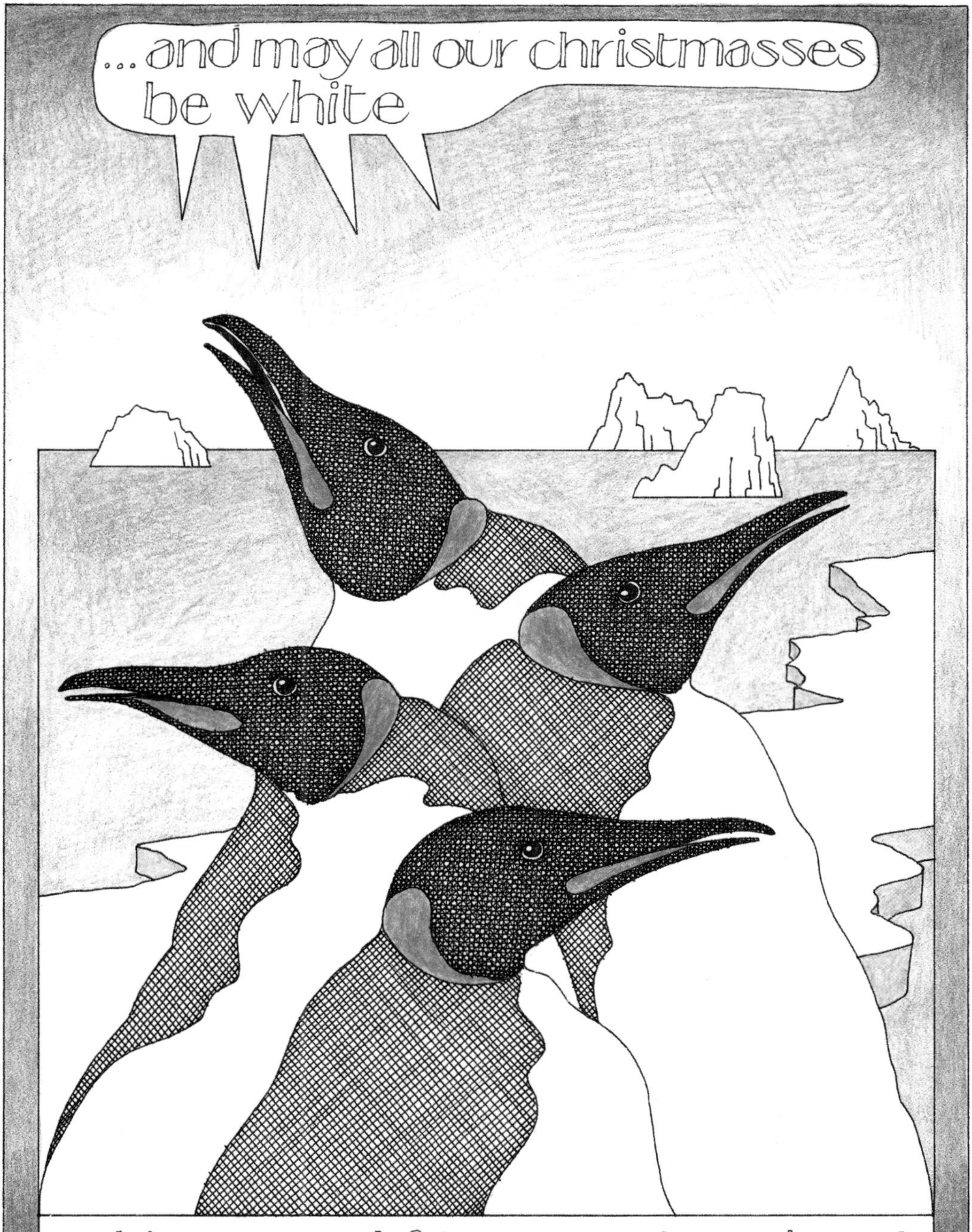

and january and february and march and

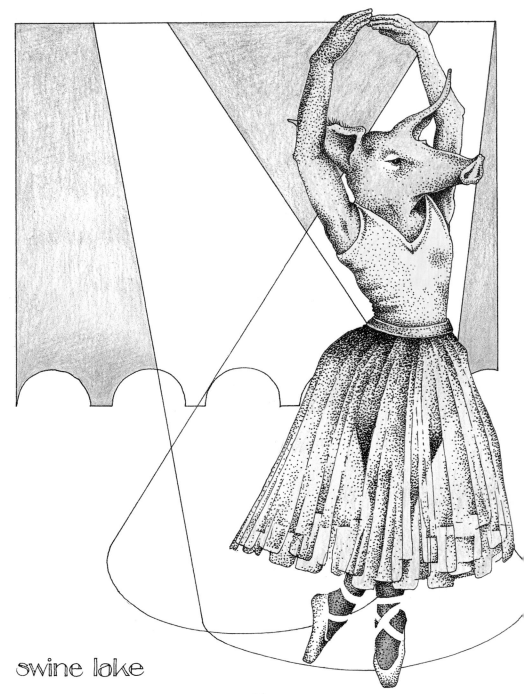

swine lake

deaf, dumb and blind

green grow the russians - O

Music in the canine world:

BEFORE

Opera: (Your tiny hound is frozen)

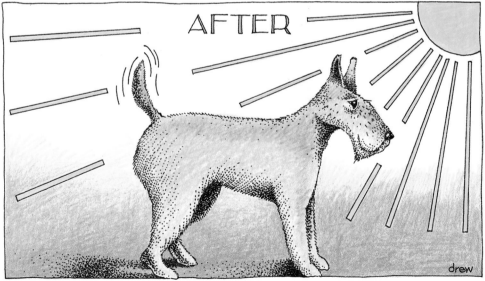

AFTER

Wagtime

Beethoven points at a
shadow of his former shelf.

the man who broke the bunk
at Monte Carlo

Joseph and his goat of many colours

Herr Strauss sitting
for his first portrait:

poor guy and bess

A German composer named Brahms
would demonstrate some of his charms:
   he'd hammer the keys
   with his elbows and knees
for his sleeves were too long for his arms.

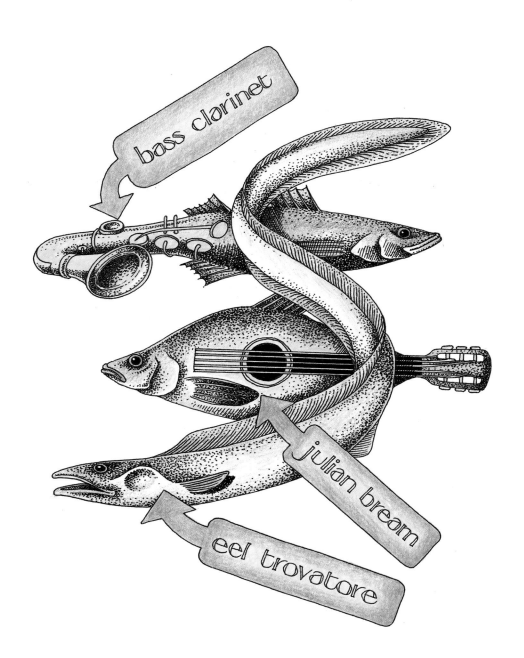

Musical Zoo

A trio of mice (that are blind) run away.
An elephant trumpets and stays.
How can a cow jump the moon
                              in the day?
And may all the sheep safely graze?
Teddy bears go to the woods
                              for their meals.
Sailors sing shanties to sprats.
Whales fill the sea with
                              melodious squeals.
And Hamelin has musical rats.

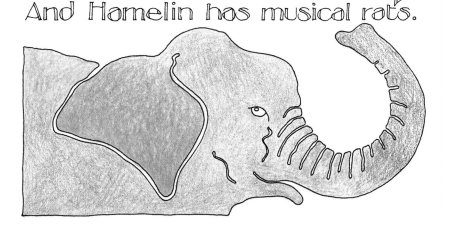

rats leaving a sinking sheep

sitting on the duck of the bay

three wise men
three wise men
see how they run
see how they run
they all ran after the eastern star -
packed all the gifts in the back of the car -
never got further than Potters Bar -
three wise men
three wise men

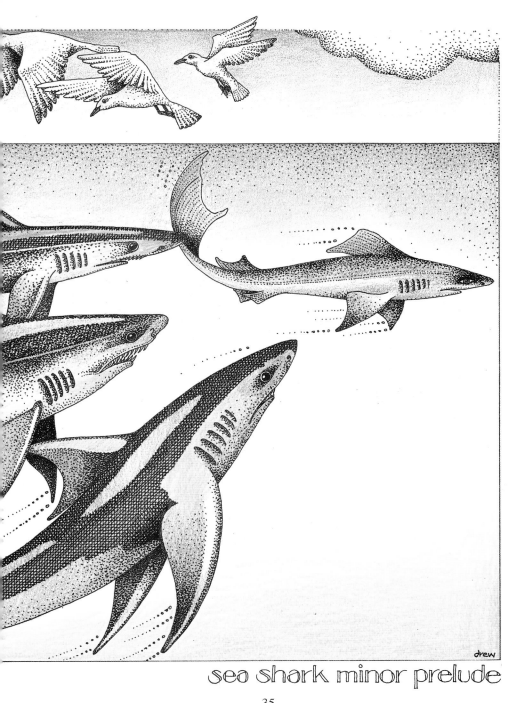

sea shark minor prelude

frank sinatra songbook part 1

strainers
in the night

hello dali

my kind of
tern, Chicago

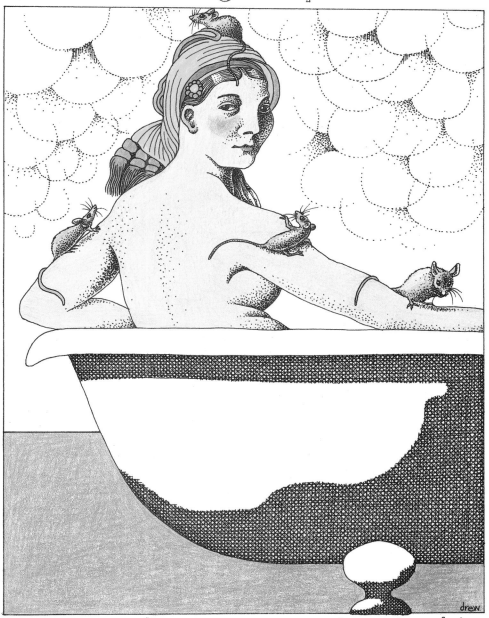

I've got you under mice kin

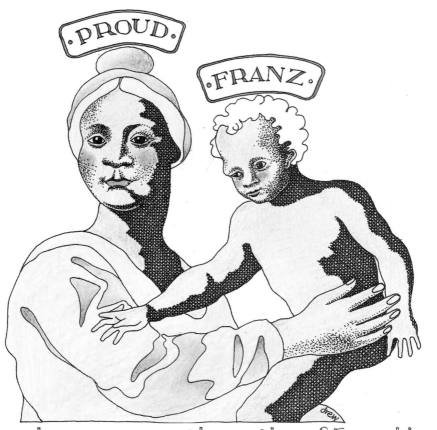

A very happy woman, the mother of Franz Liszt,
    (who often would insist
    that she never had been kissed)
    was never heard to moan or cry
    was never heard to tell a lie
    and when the people asked her why
    she gave this rather strange reply:
"If someday it may happen that an
                offspring must be found –
    I've got a little Liszt
    I've got a little Liszt."

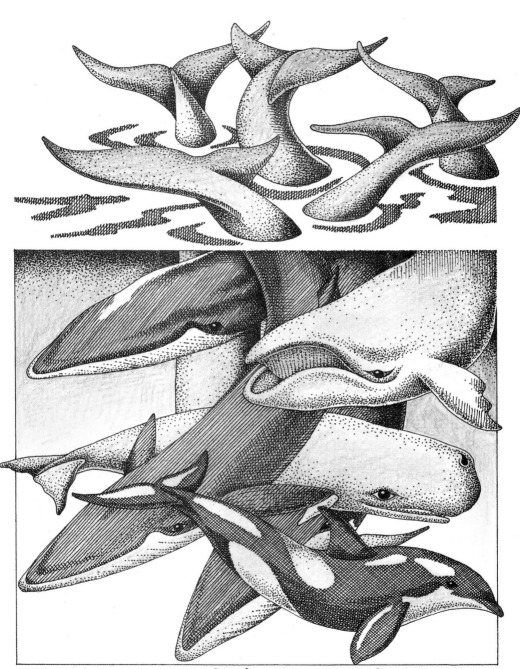

the dance of the seven whales

No movement comes from goose or cow or sheep
and farmyard sounds are muffled by the rain,
and when you think that everyone's asleep
the Bantam of the Opera sings again.

Mozart's Magic Fruit

also known as:
Liszt's Hungarian Raspberry

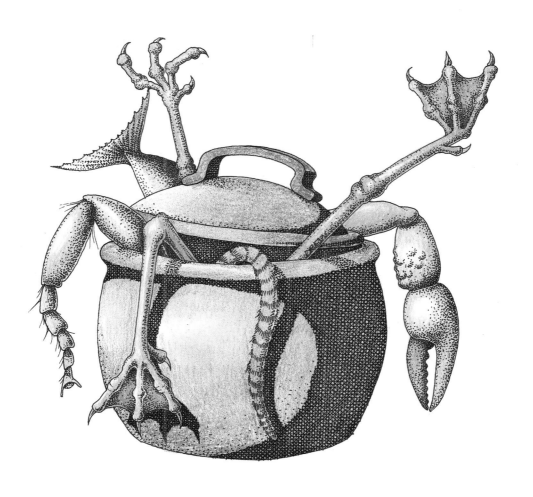

Saint-Saëns'
The Casserole of the animals

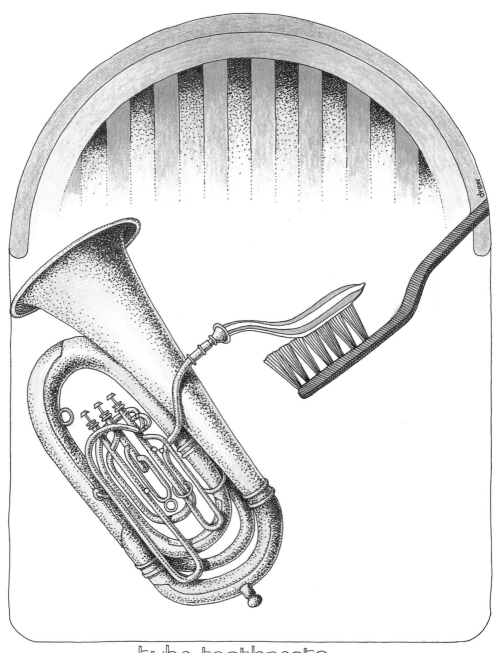

tuba toothpaste

Musorgsky's Bitches at an Exhibition

let's haul the coal thing off

the love of three orang utans

schubert's unfinished trout

drew